NEW YORK
THEN & NOW

NEW YORK
THEN & NOW

MARCIA REISS

THUNDER BAY
P·R·E·S·S

San Diego, California

Thunder Bay Press
An imprint of the Baker & Taylor Publishing Group
THUNDER BAY   10350 Barnes Canyon Road, San Diego, CA 92121
P · R · E · S · S   www.thunderbaybooks.com

Produced by Salamander Books,
an imprint of Anova Books Company Ltd.,
10 Southcombe Street, London W14 0RA, U.K.

"Then and Now" is a registered trademark of Anova Books Ltd.

© 2007 Salamander Books

All notations of errors or omissions should be addressed to Thunder Bay Press,
Editorial Department, at the above address. All other correspondence (author
inquiries, permissions) concerning the content of this book should be addressed to
Salamander Books, 10 Southcombe Street, London W14 0RA, U.K.

ISBN-13: 978-1-59223-729-6
ISBN-10: 1-59223-729-0

The Library of Congress has cataloged the original Thunder Bay edition as follows:

Reiss, Marcia.
    New York then & now / Marcia Reiss.
      p. cm.
    Third ed. of: New York then & now / Annette Witheridge. c2000.
    ISBN-13: 978-1-59223-649-7
    ISBN-10: 1-59223-649-9
    1. New York (N.Y.)--Pictorial works. 2. New York (N.Y.)--History--
Pictorial works. 3. Historic sites--New York (State)--New York--Pictorial
works. 4. New York (N.Y.)--Buildings, structures, etc.--Pictorial works.
I. Title: New York then and now. II. Witheridge, Annette. New York
then & now. III. Title.

    F128.37.W56 2006
    974.7'1--dc22
                              2005046682

Printed and bound in China
6 7 8 9 13 12 11 10

DEDICATION

To my husband, Charles Reiss, who can identify nearly every New York building and helped me peel away
the layers of history in the city's skyline.

ACKNOWLEDGMENTS

The author drew on information from the following publications:
Jackson, Kenneth T., editor, *The Encyclopedia of New York City*, Yale University Press, New Haven, 1995.
Stern, Robert A.M. and others, *New York: 1880; New York: 1960*, The Monacelli Press, New York, 1999.
Stern, Robert A.M. and others, *New York: 1900; New York: 1930*, Rizzoli International Publications, Inc.,
New York, 1983.
White, Norval and Willensky, Elliot, *AIA Guide to New York City*, Three Rivers Press, New York, 2000.
Wolfe, Gerard R., *New York: A Guide to the Metropolis*, McGraw Hill, Inc., New York, 1994.

PICTURE CREDITS

The publisher wishes to thank the following for kindly supplying the photographs that appear in this book:

Then photographs:
© CORBIS: p. 10, p. 14, p. 56, p. 126.
© Bettmann/Corbis: p. 18, p. 52, p. 54, p. 114.
© Photo Collection Alexander Alland, Sr./Corbis: p. 130.
© Collection of the New-York Historical Society: p. 1 [70587], p. 6 [50593], p. 8 [2528] p. 12 [73105], p. 16
[50741], p. 24 [57026] p. 26 (inset) [64200-493D], p. 28 [33551], p. 32 [56029], p. 42 [32183-32185], p. 48
[47587], p. 50 [44117], p. 58 [37363], p. 60 [16930], p. 62 [9229], p. 64 [49469], p. 72 [1995], p. 74 [1030],
p. 78 [49251], p. 80 [1047], p. 84 [16576], p. 86 [59171], p. 88 [59167], p. 90 [2669], p. 92 [70587], p. 94
[53661], p. 96 [60898], p. 100 [57909], p. 104 [67730], p. 110 [30634], p. 112 [57849], p. 124 [51801], p. 128
[48384], p. 134 [46150], p. 140 [32485], p. 142 [61772].
© Anova Image Library: p. 82, p. 102, p. 118, p. 136.
© Getty Images: p. 68.
© Getty Images/Hulton Archive: p. 20. p. 26, p. 44, p. 98, p. 108, p. 120, p. 138.
Library of Congress, Prints & Photographs Division: p. 22 [LC-USZ62-119537], p. 30 [LC-USZ62-96997],
p. 34 [LC-USZ62-127214], p. 36 [LC-USZ62-113332], p. 38 [HABS,NY,31-NEYO,116-1], p. 38 (inset), p.
40 [LC-USZ62-132526], p. 46 [LC-USZ62-97318], p. 66 [HABS,31-NEYO,65-2], p. 70 [LC-USZ62-
68736], p. 76 [LC-USZ62-101814], p. 106 [LC-USZ62-23866], p. 116 [LC-USZ62-103447], p. 122 [LC-
DIG-ggbain-01353], p. 132 [LC USZ62 74651].

Now photographs:
All Now images were taken by Simon Clay (© Anova Image Library) with the exception of:
© Alan Schein Photography/Corbis: p. 42, © Royalty-Free/Corbis: p. 13.

INTRODUCTION

In just a few years since the first edition of *New York Then and Now*, the city has undergone dramatic changes. The most dramatic, of course, was the result of the terrorist attack on the World Trade Center towers in 2001—the greatest tragedy in New York history and the most sudden and shocking alteration of the city's landscape. For New York City, normality is a state of constant change. Since the loss of the Twin Towers, Manhattan has continued to transform itself, as it has done since its founding four centuries ago, from a Dutch village to America's densest urban environment.

While plans for the World Trade Center site are still on the drawing board, Manhattan has experienced a building boom unlike any that came before. But it is not a matter of new buildings. Although many have gone up since 2001, much greater numbers were built in previous periods of economic prosperity. The difference now is the transformation of entire neighborhoods from industrial and commercial to residential use. Throughout the nineteenth century, this change took place in reverse, as fashionable families moved their homes uptown, escaping the intrusion of business and traffic. The pendulum is now swinging back from commercial to residential. Even more unusual, it is happening within the same buildings, as office towers, factories, and warehouses are converted to condos and luxury loft apartments.

The trend started in the 1960s in SoHo, spread to Tribeca and Wall Street in the 1980s, and is now taking place throughout the downtown area, creating distinct new residential neighborhoods like the Flatiron District, named for the tower at the forefront of office development in 1903. Most recently—and most surprising—the trend is now concentrated in Lower Manhattan around the World Trade Center site. After the heartbreak of September 11, New Yorkers have been returning not only to work but also to live in converted office towers only a short walk from Ground Zero.

This edition of *New York Then and Now* places today's cityscape within the context of history, reflecting the changing and enduring aspects of life in New York. The historic photos are fascinating revelations of the way New Yorkers lived, worked, and moved about the city, how they entertained themselves and endured hardship and even tragedy. The chaotic scene of the Wall Street bombing of 1920 now looks like a somber precursor to September 11. Together with the current photo of luxury condos on the same Wall Street corner, it also reveals New York's amazing resilience.

The city advanced through a series of prodigious achievements. The Croton Aqueduct brought clean drinking water from an upstate source to a massive reservoir in the middle of Manhattan in 1842, greatly improving the health of its citizens. Central Park, St. Patrick's Cathedral, and Grand Central Station expanded the city northward, shaping its raw edge into elegant neighborhoods and thriving business districts. Many incredible undertakings progressed in the midst of earthshaking events. Central Park and St. Patrick's were interrupted but not derailed by the Civil War. Rockefeller Center, the city's largest private real estate venture, was built during the worst years of the Depression. Some of the biggest projects were built simultaneously: Penn Station, Grand Central Terminal, and the Woolworth Building, then the world's tallest, were all completed by 1913. The Empire State Building and the George Washington Bridge both opened in 1931.

In 1892, the year the Protestant establishment broke ground for its masterpiece, the Cathedral of St. John the Divine, waves of immigrants began to pass through Ellis Island, forever changing the face and culture of the city's neighborhoods. Sixteen million immigrants were processed through Ellis Island from 1892 to 1924. Their lives are reflected in the photos of St. Patrick's Cathedral, built with the pennies of Irish immigrants; the Columbus Circle Monument, erected by Italian Americans; and Lower East Side streets crowded with the pushcarts of Jewish merchants from eastern Europe.

New York's signature skyscrapers flourished in Lower Manhattan in the first decades of the twentieth century. Vertical buildings were an efficient way to build office space on these narrow streets. But as tower after tower rose in Midtown, Manhattan's widest point, it became increasingly clear that efficiency was not the driving force. Prestige, pride, and power pushed corporations to aim for the sky. Architects envisioned a city of towers in splendid isolation, but layers of modern development now make it hard to identify all but the most distinctive ones within the skyline—the Chrysler and Empire State buildings.

The historic photos display many other extraordinary buildings. Development of the elevator, telephone, and electric lighting in the late nineteenth century produced not only skyscrapers but also palatial department stores and the largest and most lavish hotels in the city's history. Macy's, Wanamaker's and Saks Fifth Avenue were built to serve the rising middle class. The first Waldorf-Astoria and the famed Plaza Hotel became meeting places for the rich and famous. Even factories and warehouses, like the cast-iron survivors in SoHo and Tribeca, were designed with grand aspirations.

One of New York's magnificent buildings, Penn Station, was demolished in 1963 for a mundane replacement, an inconceivable act of destruction today. The loss led to the city's first landmark protection law for other great buildings—Grand Central Terminal, the Jefferson Market Courthouse, and many others within these pages. Today, New York is an astounding mix of old and new, an ever-changing picture of a dynamic city.

Artist Albert Bierstadt made this photo print in 1890, four years after the Statue of Liberty was erected in New York Harbor. Titled *Liberty Enlightening the World*, the monument was first conceived in 1865, during the reign of Napoléon III, by a group of French Republicans who were eager to focus attention on the upcoming centennial of France's support for American independence. The colossal figure became a stirring symbol of welcome to millions of immigrants. In 1903 a plaque was installed inside the pedestal, bearing the now-famous lines by Emma Lazarus: "Give me your tired, your poor, your huddled masses yearning to breathe free . . ." The statue was designed by sculptor Frederic Auguste Bartholdi, who used his mother's face as a model for Liberty's and his then-mistress (and future wife) for the statue's arms. The steel skeleton was engineered by Alexandre Gustave Eiffel, who designed the Eiffel Tower in 1889.

The statue got a total makeover for its centennial on July 4, 1986. French artisans came to New York to work on the statue, as their countrymen had done a century before. Once seen as the symbol of a French-American alliance, the statue is clearly an American icon and the French connection is only a subtext today. Closed after the World Trade Center attacks on September 11, 2001, it did not reopen until August 2004. The monumental pedestal, as tall as the statue, has a glass ceiling that affords views into the figure, but the public can no longer ascend the interior staircase to her spiked crown. Her arm and torch have been off-limits since 1916 after German saboteurs exploded a cache of dynamite on a nearby wharf, which resulted in some bolts getting lodged in the arm and weakening the structure.

Dutch settlers landed here at the southern tip of Manhattan in 1623, but by the time of this 1883 photo, the water's edge was packed with urban buildings. The circular structure is Castle Clinton, built as a fort to deter the British from attacking New York in the War of 1812. It first stood on a rocky outcrop some 200 feet offshore, and became part of Manhattan when the waterfront was extended around it by landfill. Remodeled as a concert hall and renamed Castle Garden, it became famous in 1850 for hosting the "musical event of the century," the debut of Jenny Lind, "the Swedish Nightingale." Five years later, it gave up its starring role to become the Emigrant Landing Depot, where some eight million new Americans were processed. Ellis Island took over that job in 1892. Castle Clinton found new life in 1896 as the city's aquarium, which was housed there until 1941.

Castle Clinton and all of Battery Park were nearly destroyed in the 1940s by a plan to build a bridge from this spot to Brooklyn. They were saved at the last minute by a public outcry that transformed the project into the Brooklyn–Battery Tunnel. The old fort was stripped of its roof and aquarium but was preserved as a national monument (inset). It is also visible within the trees, just to the right of the excursion boat, and now serves as the place to buy tickets for excursions to the Statue of Liberty and Ellis Island. Musical performances returned in 1997 with a Castle Clinton concert series, the first since the last performance in 1854. Many of the buildings in the background were built as headquarters for shipping companies a century ago, when this area was known as Steamship Row.

Once fortified with a battery of guns, Manhattan's southern shoreline was used as a public promenade from as early as 1790. By the time of this 1906 photo, it was a popular esplanade bordered by the manicured lawns of Battery Park. Castle Clinton, the round building in the far right background, was operating at this time as the New York Aquarium. The structure immediately to its left is Pier A, a long, covered dock with a peaked tower at the end. This was New York's formal reception pier, where city officials greeted important visitors arriving by ship.

The boardwalk was officially named the Admiral Dewey Promenade in 1973, the seventy-fifth anniversary of Dewey's victory in the Spanish-American War. Today, the panoramic views take in towering buildings on both sides of the harbor. Those on the left are in New Jersey. On the right are the latest additions to Battery Park City, just north of the park. Castle Clinton's circular brick walls can be seen within the trees. After years of neglect, all of Battery Park, the historic site of the Dutch settlement of New Amsterdam, is sprouting beautiful gardens created by the Dutch landscape designer Piet Oudolf. Pier A is also being restored as a visitor center and restaurant.

On the day this photo was taken, January 21, 1934, the nation was in the depths of the Great Depression. But New York City still presented an impressive skyline, created in the building boom of the early twentieth century, when the skyscraper became the city's signature. The spires of several famous ones stand out. On the left are the Woolworth (1913) and Singer (1909) buildings, and in the center is the seventy-one-story Bank of Manhattan Building (1930), the tallest structure in Lower Manhattan. To the far right are the pylons of three spans over the East River: the Brooklyn, Manhattan, and Williamsburg bridges. Castle Clinton, the low circular building along the shoreline, can also be seen in the midst of Battery Park.

Much bigger and bulkier than in 1934, the skyline has been totally reshaped by development, new architectural styles, and tragic events. The skyline's former peak, the World Trade Center towers (inset), is gone, but a wall of other office towers built in the 1970s and 1980s still obscures most of the earlier skyscrapers. The blue pyramid roof of the former Bank of Manhattan Building, now the Trump Building at 40 Wall Street, is barely visible just right of center. A bit farther on the right is a blue, curved glass tower built in 1989 on the site, now 17 State Street, where author Herman Melville was born in 1819. Melville's birthplace is not far from where Dutch colonial administrator Peter Stuyvesant's mansion stood at One State Street two centuries earlier.

As the nation's center of trade, New York garnered the lion's share of U.S. customs duties at this imposing Beaux-Arts building, completed in 1907 in the heart of Lower Manhattan. Seen here in 1915, it was the achievement of a little-known architect from Minnesota, Cass Gilbert, who soon went on to design the Woolworth Building. Better known at the time than the architect, the chief sculptor of the Custom House, Daniel Chester French, created the monumental statues at the entrance, symbolizing the four continents of Asia, America, Europe, and Africa. French later designed the figure of Abraham Lincoln in the Lincoln Memorial in Washington, D.C.

The preserved exterior belies dramatic changes inside the building. After the 1950s, shipping through the Port of New York declined as the steamship companies relocated from Manhattan piers to new, larger facilities in New Jersey. Unable to maintain the lavish building, U.S. Customs moved in 1977 to modern quarters a few blocks to the north in the new World Trade Center, completed the year before.

Empty for many years, the Custom House finally took in a new tenant, the National Museum of the American Indian, housing a vast collection of Indian artifacts from North, Central, and South America. Surrounded by office towers and adorned by sculpture extolling international trade, the building now celebrates Native American history prior to European settlement.

The street takes its name from a wooden wall built here by the Dutch in 1653 as protection against attack by English colonies to the north—a threat that never materialized. The name became famous after 1865 when the New York Stock Exchange established its permanent home at Wall and Broad streets, the intersection shown here. Although the Exchange building is not visible in this 1870 photo, its influence had already made the name "Wall Street" synonymous with high-powered finance. This view shows the street's other historic buildings: Trinity Church, the tallest structure in Lower Manhattan at this time, and, on the right, the steps of Federal Hall.

Nestled comfortably within a canyon of skyscrapers, Trinity Church is still one of the city's most famous landmarks. The first version was built on this site at the head of Wall Street in 1698 as a colonial outpost of the English Anglican Church. It burned down in 1776, in a fire most likely started by American rebels during the British occupation of New York City in the Revolutionary War. The fire consumed some 500 buildings in Lower Manhattan, about a third of the city at the time. A second church was constructed in 1790 and demolished in 1839. This version, by architect Richard Upjohn, was built in 1856 in the English Gothic style. The fence in the middle of the street was erected to restrict traffic for security reasons after September 11, 2001.

On September 16, 1920, at the corner of Wall and Broad streets—the hub of American capitalism—a horse-drawn cart exploded into the noontime crowd. The blast killed forty people, mostly clerks and stenographers on their lunch breaks, and wounded hundreds more. Those responsible for the violence were never discovered, although it was widely thought to be the act of anarchists. Eager to subdue fears of a stock market crash, financial leaders dispatched a battalion of sweepers and repairmen who worked through the night to remove the rubble and bloodstains from the street. The next day, Wall Street workers, many bearing bandages, were called back to their offices, and the street returned to business as usual.

Although the bombing that rocked this corner in 1920 left permanent scars on the stonework of one corner building, this early terrorist act has faded from memory. Thousands of office workers and tourists come here each day, caught up in the fast pace of the financial district. The statue of George Washington, erected in 1883 on the spot where he was inaugurated as the first U.S. president in 1789, weathered the bombing without a scratch and still presides over America's center of free enterprise. The building behind the statue, Federal Hall, a magnificent Greek Revival edifice built in 1842, also survived without damage.

The two buildings on either side of Broad Street in this 1930s view were the bedrock of the financial district: J. P. Morgan & Company on the left and the New York Stock Exchange on the right. While skyscrapers were rising all around it in Lower Manhattan, the Morgan bank confined its headquarters to an austere, four-story building completed in 1913, the same year the sixty-story Woolworth Building opened. Like a prestigious club, the bank had no name on its exterior. Those wealthy enough to bank there knew where to find it. Across the street is the New York Stock Exchange with its six monumental Corinthian columns. Housed in a number of sites in the area since its founding in 1817, the Stock Exchange moved into this grand building in 1903.

Although J. P. Morgan knowingly passed up the opportunity to build an office tower on this choice spot, developers are taking full advantage of it as a prime residential location. In 2005, the Morgan building became a house of luxury condos, forming the grand entrance to a residential tower behind it. The building is called Downtown by Phillipe Starck after its trendy interior designer. Affluent buyers grabbed up the multimillion-dollar condos, even though the Stock Exchange across the street was declared a terrorist target during the sales period. Real estate wags have dubbed the area the "Starck Exchange." The stone wall of the Morgan building still bears a few pockmarks from the 1920 bombing at this corner.

The crowd of people in this 1916 photo were "curb brokers" who traded stocks on the street. Waving hand signals frantically, they conveyed buy or sell orders to clerks in nearby buildings. The practice harks back to 1790, when brokers gathered in outdoor markets to trade government bonds covering debts incurred during the American Revolution. The New York Stock Exchange with its Greek-columned facade is just up the street on the left. To its left is the Bankers Trust Company Building at 14 Wall Street, the tower topped by tall, arched windows. Completed in 1912, it was considered the world's tallest structure on the smallest plot of land.

LOOKING NORTH ON BROAD STREET

The curb exchange moved to the American Stock Exchange on nearby Trinity Place in 1921. The same hand signals were still used inside the AMEX Building for decades. Broad Street began in Dutch colonial times as a wide canal extending to the East River. Lined with open markets, it was filled in as a street in 1676. A center of finance ever since the New York Stock Exchange first arrived here in 1865, the street is now going through another period of change. Like several other historic office buildings on Broad Street, the towering Bankers Trust, shown here with its pyramid roof, will soon be converted to residential condos. Federal Hall's Greek Revival facade can be seen at the head of the street in both photos.

Best known for its theater district uptown, Broadway extends along the entire length of Manhattan, and continues northward to Albany and beyond in upstate New York. This section in Lower Manhattan was one of the busiest parts of the city when this photo was taken in 1887. Originally an American Indian trail, the street is lined with horse-drawn carriages and trolley tracks. The steeple of Trinity Church at the intersection of Broadway and Wall Street dominates the view. Several blocks up the street, the tower of the Western Union Building also stands out amid this low skyline. A tangle of electrical wires crosses the sky, but just a year later, the Great Blizzard of 1888 wreaked such havoc that the city required all the overhead lines to be buried underground.

Trinity Church is no longer the tallest structure on Broadway, yet its Gothic architecture stands out even more among the modern buildings. Behind the church is the white Trinity Building, erected in 1907 with Gothic detailing to harmonize with the church. Looming over them is One Liberty Plaza, a steel-faced giant of the 1970s. Cars have replaced the carriages, and instead of trolley tracks, subways run deep underground. War heroes, astronauts, baseball champions, and other celebrities have paraded through streams of ticker tape along this "Canyon of Heroes."

Two buildings, adjacent but very different in architectural form, are in construction in the 1907 view, above, and just completed in this 1908 view, left. The taller one is the tower of the Singer Building. Immediately in front of it is the wider City Investing Building. The Singer Sewing Machine Company had previously built a ten-story building on this site, designed by Ernest Flagg. When the company learned that City Investing was planning to build a huge structure next door, they hired Flagg to design a distinctive tower above the base of their old building. Flagg created a slender, freestanding tower that made the Singer Building the city's tallest for a short time. Even after other buildings surpassed its height, the Singer Building's Second Empire Baroque profile became one of New York's best known and most admired landmarks.

The architects of the Singer and City Investing buildings could not have imagined the hulking black edifice that would replace them in 1974. Although the demolition of City Investing brought little opposition, the loss of the Singer tower led to an outcry from preservationists. But no matter how supporters praised its graceful form, the slender tower could not compete with the U.S. Steel Building, which offered nearly ten times more rentable office space. The Singer Building was demolished in 1968, just as the World Trade Center towers were rising across the street. Ironically, the trade center created a glut of office space, making it hard to rent out Lower Manhattan buildings for more than a decade. The Singer was the tallest building ever demolished, until the Twin Towers were destroyed on September 11, 2001.

Towering over the area, the Western Union Telegraph Company Building was constructed in 1875 and became New York City's tallest commercial building. Midday crowds often gathered outside to watch a ball descend from the top of the pole above the clock tower, precisely at noon. The flamboyant Renaissance-style building housed the latest equipment for the rapidly expanding communications company. The sixth floor was the battery room that powered the telegraphs and served as the point of entry for the company's wires. On the seventh floor was a huge switchboard manned by nearly 300 operators, both men and women, separated by a tall partition. Inside the mansard roof, just beneath the clock tower, were the offices of the New York Associated Press, connected by telegraph to the latest happenings around the country.

Outdated by the start of the twentieth century, the old Western Union Building on Broadway was demolished. After several moves, the company eventually relocated in 1930 to a massive Art Deco building at 60 Hudson Street. The large white structure in this view was built by a competing communications giant, the American Telephone and Telegraph Corporation, which acquired control of Western Union in 1909, but an antitrust ruling soon separated the two companies. The AT&T Building went up at 195 Broadway in three sections between 1912 and 1923, with more classical columns than any facade in the world. AT&T left these headquarters in 1984 for a Philip Johnson–designed postmodernist tower with a Chippendale top on Madison Avenue and Fifty-fifth Street.

This 1916 photo shows new buildings encroaching on the old intersection of Broadway, Fulton, and Vesey streets. On the right is the Astor Building, an office building erected in 1914 to replace the Astor House, a hotel built in 1836. By the time of this photo, the Astors were operating their much grander Waldorf-Astoria Hotel in a more fashionable neighborhood uptown. The low building in the center is the portico of St. Paul's Chapel, built as a northern outpost of Trinity Church in 1766, a time when rough roads between the two churches made for a difficult trip. Trolley cars are providing much easier travel in this view. To the left of St. Paul's is the Victorian-style Evening Mail Building. The large white building rising above it is the first section of the AT&T Building, completed in 1912 at 195 Broadway.

The Astor Building and St. Paul's, obscured by trees, still stand at this busy intersection, hemmed in by a continuing wave of development since the earlier photo. The white building to the left of St. Paul's is the second section of the AT&T Building, which replaced the Evening Mail Building in 1923. The trolleys are gone, leaving no trace of their tracks. The old trolley turnaround is landscaped with natural plants, and a red double-decker tour bus is heading south on Broadway, now smoothly paved. An antique-style streetlight adds a touch of history. The photo above, taken prior to September 11, 2001, shows the church's proximity to the World Trade Center.

This cast-iron footbridge was built over Broadway in 1866 to allow pedestrians to cross the impossibly crowded streets. Horse-drawn vehicles of every kind—carts, wagons, private carriages, and public streetcars—clogged the street and kept customers from reaching local shops. A hatter with a shop at the Fulton Street intersection had persuaded the city's Common Council to build the bridge. However, after the hatter's competitor across the street claimed that the bridge blocked light to his store and attracted loiterers, the council agreed to take it down. The handsome portico of St. Paul's Chapel is visible above the bridge.

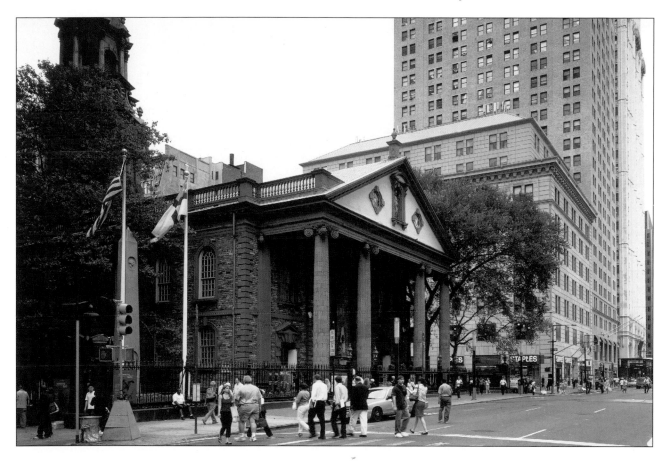

A constant flow of traffic still passes by St. Paul's. But this stately building, where English lords and George Washington worshipped two centuries ago, has remained an active church—never more so than for the nine months after September 11, 2001, when it was open twenty-four hours a day as a respite center for rescue workers. The World Trade Center towers stood close behind the chapel. When they collapsed, the church was miraculously spared. President Washington attended services here during the brief period after the Revolution when New York City was the nation's capital. The original U.S. presidential seal still hangs on the wall above his pew.

Just beginning its seventeen-year reign as the world's tallest structure, the newly completed Woolworth Building towers above Broadway and City Hall Park in this 1913 view. It was created by F. W. Woolworth, the founder of the five-and-dime store chain, and Cass Gilbert, architect of the U.S. Custom House. Called "the Cathedral of Commerce," it has Gothic pointed arches, making the building soar to a pinnacled crown. Taken from the northeast, the photo shows the roof of City Hall in the center foreground and, on the left, the domed post office that once dominated City Hall Park. Critics called the massive post office "a boil on the end of a man's nose" because it blocked views of the park and City Hall. It was demolished in the 1930s.

Like all great skyscrapers, the Woolworth Building's height, sixty stories, was not the only reason for its lasting fame. It lost its title as the world's tallest building to the Chrysler Building in 1930 and was dwarfed by the World Trade Center towers (above) in the 1970s. Although the towers look quite close, they were several blocks away and their fall did not damage the Woolworth Building. Modernist architects in the 1950s disdained the Woolworth's ornate neo-Gothic facade, but after decades of spare, modern buildings, they have been proved wrong. Frank Woolworth paid more than $13 million—in cash—to construct the building. His company retained ownership for eighty-five years before finally selling it in 1998 for $155 million. Today, the building is valued even more highly by developers who are planning to convert these unique offices to luxury condos.

In this 1919 view, City Hall looks much the way it did when it was completed in 1811—no small feat, since there had been serious efforts to demolish and totally redesign the building at the end of the nineteenth century. In one of the city's earliest historic preservation campaigns, a group of old-line New Yorkers convinced government officials that demolishing City Hall would be an "act of vandalism."

Although the building survived, its condition deteriorated for many years. Shortly after this photo was taken, a fire nearly destroyed the cupola and copper dome. Its original marble exterior eroded and the rear of the building, covered in cheaper brownstone, remained unfinished for decades. A statue of Nathan Hale, an American patriot hanged by the British in the Revolutionary War, stands in front of the building.

City Hall's marble exterior was finally replaced by limestone in the 1950s, and, this time, the white facade also covered the building's brownstone back. The historic interior has been beautifully restored in more recent years. The small, elegant building is still the center of government, where New York City's mayor and city council conduct their daily business as they have done for nearly two centuries. However, security threats after September 11 have made the building off-limits to the public. Fenced and heavily guarded, it is open only to those on official business. Even Nathan Hale's statue had to be moved and now stands in City Hall Park.

The courthouse is informally named for William "Boss" Tweed, the corrupt political powerhouse who controlled New York City government from the 1860s to the early 1870s. A rotund figure who wore a large diamond in his shirtfront, Tweed was the king of kickbacks. He extracted millions of dollars from contractors by grossly inflating the costs of public projects. He and his cronies made off with ten of the fourteen million dollars expended for the courthouse. By the time the courthouse was built in 1872, the scheme was uncovered and exposed in the newspapers. A year later, Tweed was tried and convicted in this very building; he died in prison in 1878. This view shows the once-elaborate building after its front steps had been removed in order to widen the street. Its thirty ornate courtrooms (inset) were also in a state of disrepair.

Handsomely restored with a grand staircase in 2003, the former courthouse has regained its dignity and taken on a new purpose. Its courtrooms and rotunda, grown shabby throughout their years as city offices, have been beautifully refurbished for the Department of Education and City Hall Academy, a new school offering enriched programs for students and teachers. In an ironic tribute to Tweed, the building known by his name and tainted by his corruption is now recognized as one of the greatest achievements in the city's array of civic architecture. The Municipal Building (1914) is visible here in the background on the left, as in the earlier photo.

The horizontal structure in this 1911 view is the Manhattan Terminal of the Brooklyn Bridge, an elevated station for the electric trains and trolley cars that crossed the bridge. Trains replaced the original cable car system in 1898, and by 1907, sixty trains an hour were running across the bridge. The terminal was enlarged several times, projecting beyond Park Row into City Hall Park. Rising above the station is the construction of the Municipal Building, a twenty-five-story skyscraper that would not be completed for another three years. It would provide expansion room for the multitude of offices squeezed into City Hall.

Trains eventually gave way to cars on the bridge and the old terminal was dismantled in 1944. Today, the number of city offices has outgrown the Municipal Building and they have spread throughout the five boroughs. But among its remaining services, the building still holds civil marriages, and wedding parties are a common sight in City Hall Park. Once the site of a prison, poorhouse, and gunpowder warehouse, the park was recently restored and is a welcome green oasis within the busy civic center.

The Manhattan tower of the bridge was built in 1876, the year this amazing picture (above) was taken, seven years before the span and cables were finally strung across the river. The photo was taken from the top of the tower on the Brooklyn side that went up first. The Manhattan tower proved more difficult to build, as workers had to dig down nearly eighty feet under the river before reaching a stable foundation, almost twice the depth for the Brooklyn tower. This difficult and dangerous work was done in huge, airtight caissons. Changing air pressure in these underwater shafts often caused painful cases of the bends, and sometimes death. Rising more than 276 feet above water, the Manhattan tower dominates the city skyline. The large domed building in the left background is the old post office in City Hall Park, completed just a year before this photo was taken.

Seen from the bridge today (left), Manhattan is a completely different city. The World Trade Center towers once dominated this view, but even without their presence, the skyline is all skyscrapers. Only a few slender spires from the early skyscraper era remain in this wall of blocklike towers. The East River waterfront is no longer an active port, but a few tall-masted ships are still docked at the South Street Seaport, preserving a bit of New York's maritime history. Outlined in lights at the river's edge is the Seaport's Pier 17 Pavilion. Built in the 1980s and filled with shops and restaurants, it has become a new waterfront landmark.

This photo was taken on January 1, 1884, less than a year after the bridge opened in May 1883. First proposed in 1857 by German-born engineer John Augustus Roebling, construction of the bridge finally got underway in 1869. He was killed in an accident shortly afterward, and his son, Washington Roebling, carried on the demanding work. Injured in one of the caissons, the younger Roebling became an invalid and, with his wife's help, supervised the project from his bedside window across the river in Brooklyn. It took fourteen years to complete and cost $16 million, three times the original estimate and more than any other single endeavor of the day. Its cables were spun from steel, a material still new in the mid-nineteenth century.

Except for a few tall buildings on the Brooklyn side and the absence of ship masts in the foreground, this scene is nearly identical to the earlier photo. A wondrous achievement in its day, the bridge has proved itself in the modern world with relatively few changes. Nineteenth-century New Yorkers, crossing on cable cars, horse-drawn trolleys, and electric trains, could not have imagined how the bridge would prove adaptable to motorized vehicles. For the first seventy years of its life, well into the period of the automobile, the bridge required only routine maintenance. In 1953, the deck was strengthened to bear the weight of increased motor traffic. Although no longer the largest or most innovative, the bridge still captures one's imagination for its grace and beauty.

From the day it opened, the bridge attracted a steady flow of pedestrians eager to experience the new phenomenon. A tragic accident occurred on Memorial Day 1883, just a week after the opening. In the crush of an uncontrollably large crowd on the stairway leading to the bridge, panic broke out and twelve people were trampled to death. The number of police officers on the bridge was increased and pedestrians, including thousands who walked to work to save on the cable car fare, continued to use it. Many others, like these handsomely dressed New Yorkers, came to enjoy a stroll over the city's highest structure. In this image, a woman is clutching her long skirt to keep it from getting dirty on the walkway. A year after the accident, impresario P. T. Barnum marched a herd of twenty-one elephants over the bridge to demonstrate its solidity.

A new generation of walkers, runners, and bicyclists have made the bridge so popular that a yellow line had to be painted down the center of the walkway to keep them from bumping into each other. Many Brooklynites continue to walk to work and back home over the bridge. At lunchtime it becomes a running track for office workers. Despite the noise from cars driving on the roadway twelve feet below, crossing the bridge on foot or bicycle is one of the city's great experiences. The powerful cables and stone arches frame fascinating views of the city.

As a city of islands, New York's lifeline was its arterial network of ferries. Before and even after the bridges were built, dozens of ferry lines plied the waters between Manhattan and the other New York boroughs. Beginning in the early nineteenth century, the Fulton Ferry line—named for Robert Fulton, the inventor of the steam-powered ferry—was the busiest service between Manhattan and Brooklyn.

This photograph of the Manhattan terminal on South Street was taken in 1876, the year the Manhattan tower of the Brooklyn Bridge was completed nearby. While the opening of the bridge in 1883 reduced the number of passengers, the Fulton Ferry continued to operate for another twenty years.

This new terminal is evidence of a resurgence in ferry service to Manhattan after a hiatus of more than fifty years. Except for the Staten Island Ferry, all lines stopped running after World War II. By the end of the twentieth century, with cars clogging bridges and tunnels and polluting the air, federal funds became available for new ferry terminals. Jutting out from East River Drive, the sleek pier built at Wall and South streets in 2000 (with inset shot looking shoreward from the pier) provides dock space for private lines between Manhattan, New Jersey, Brooklyn, and Queens. Although the service is still only a fraction of the traffic into Manhattan, many Wall Street office commuters now enjoy a refreshing boat ride to work and back instead of a bumper-to-bumper commute. In this photo, a police boat and helicopter are providing security for President George W. Bush's arrival at the neighboring helicopter pier on September 13, 2005.

South Street from the Battery to Fulton Street was the heart of the Port of New York for most of the nineteenth century. Tall-masted sailing ships like these lined this stretch of the East River waterfront, and their spars and jibs nearly touched the buildings across the street. It was a crowded, rowdy neighborhood of maritime shops, boarding houses, saloons, and brothels. Filled with the sounds and smells of the sea, it was packed with ships, horses, wagons, and men of every shipping trade, all jostling for space. This view is from the 1890s, a time when larger oceangoing vessels were moving to new docks and deeper water on the Hudson River along Manhattan's West Side.

A small fleet of historic ships docked at the foot of South and Fulton streets preserves a sense of the old port. The *Peking*, built in Germany in 1911, and the *Wavertree*, built in England in 1885, are always docked here for public view. The *Ambrose* lightship, once anchored at sea to guide ships entering the harbor, is another permanent resident. The ships are part of the South Street Seaport Historic District, which covers three piers and a dozen blocks south of the Brooklyn Bridge. New restaurants and shops fill new and old buildings, some from the early nineteenth century. Not all modern hype, this merchandising mecca recalls the shops that opened here in the early 1800s to serve throngs of passengers taking the Fulton Ferry.

A few blocks west of City Hall, the Washington Market complex was originally built in 1812 and by 1858 had become the largest food market in the country. Rife with corruption, it was shut down by the city in 1859. At the end of the Civil War, a wholesale produce market sprouted several blocks to the north at North Moore Street. The original food market was rebuilt on Washington Street in the 1880s and is seen here in about 1900. Shipments of fruits and vegetables came directly to the market by trains, which rode the tracks in these cobblestone streets. Men on horseback preceded the trains, warning pedestrians to move out of the way.

The city closed the retail market in 1956 and sent the wholesale produce market up to a new facility in the Bronx. The entire market area was consumed in an urban renewal project that cleared more than a dozen blocks from North Moore to Liberty Street in the 1960s. In the following years, the area was transformed into a city of new development, including the World Trade Center, Independence Plaza apartment towers, Manhattan Community College, a park, and this public elementary school, P.S. 234. The only evidence of the old market is the park's name, Washington Market Park, and several small plaques on the side of the school, featuring pictures of the old market.

The newly completed World Trade Center towers were the stars of the New York waterfront on July 4, 1976, the day of this photo. A fleet of tall ships from around the world filled the waters surrounding Manhattan for Operation Sail, the highlight of the Bicentennial celebration. The Twin Towers were part of the seven-building World Trade Center complex. Japanese architect Minoru Yamasaki began designing the complex in 1962, and the first buildings opened in 1970. The Twin Towers, each 110 stories in height, opened in 1976, becoming the tallest buildings in the world and redefining the Manhattan skyline.

The excavation for the Twin Towers in the 1970s created an enormous volume of landfill, adding ninety-two acres to Lower Manhattan's Hudson River shoreline. The new swath of Manhattan became the development shown here: Battery Park City and the World Financial Center, a residential and office complex of astounding size and distinguished architectural design built in the 1980s. The Twin Towers once rose above this line of buildings, many of which were damaged in the September 11, 2001, attacks. Residents had to be evacuated, and some could not return to their ash-filled apartments for six months or more. Although the skyline has changed dramatically, the area is a vibrant community once again.

In the early twentieth century, a generation after the wonder of the Brooklyn Bridge, suspension bridges over the East River were becoming a more common sight. Still under construction in this view, the Manhattan Bridge, the third suspension bridge to span the river between Manhattan and Brooklyn, was completed in 1909. Like its predecessor, the Williamsburg Bridge (1903), its towers were made not of stone, the material used for the Brooklyn Bridge towers (1883), but of steel. While the bridge would soon provide quicker passage, a ferry can still be seen crossing the river.

The completed bridge looks much the same, but like the neighborhood at its base, it has undergone many changes over the years. Despite its more modern steel construction, it did not hold up nearly as well as the Brooklyn Bridge. From the start, it was designed to carry a much heavier load—four subway tracks. It showed signs of strain in the 1940s, and by 1978, after years of inadequate maintenance, serious cracks were discovered. The city considered tearing it down and replacing it, but instead embarked on a long-term, intensive repair project, periodically shutting down several sections for years at a time. The project is scheduled to be completed in 2006, after $646 million in repairs.

This was the main shopping area of the most crowded neighborhood in the city—the Lower East Side. While Manhattan as a whole was densely settled by this period of the 1890s, averaging more than 100 residents per acre, the Lower East Side averaged more than 500 people per acre. Thousands of immigrant families were packed into tenements.

The building exteriors looked like typical row houses, but the families inside endured closer quarters than did city dwellers anywhere else in the world, including the slums of London, China, and India. People filled the streets, shopping for food from pushcarts and finding some relief outdoors from their crowded living conditions.

Hester Street's boarded-up storefronts reflect a neighborhood in transition (inset). The intersection of Hester and Norfolk streets is now in the middle of Seward Park Houses, which includes this park surrounded by residential buildings. The development was built in 1960 by the International Ladies Garment Workers Union, the savior of the Lower East Side sweatshop workers. Former tenement dwellers, whose parents did "piecework" sewing in their overcrowded homes, moved to modern apartments in the new buildings. The aging population is now being replaced by a later generation of immigrants from China, Puerto Rico, and other countries. Only a few blocks away, young professionals are moving into high-priced apartments, shopping at fashionable boutiques, and hanging out in hip clubs and restaurants.

Hudson, like Water, Canal, and other New York streets with maritime names, took its name from its proximity to the water. Extended by landfill over centuries of development, the Manhattan shoreline was changed by waves of new activity. The shops in these rough brick buildings at the southern end of Hudson Street most likely started out as adjuncts to the shipping trade. But the workers in this 1865 view—carpenters, printers, sign painters, and pharmacists—are now jacks-of-all-trades. By the end of the nineteenth century, these buildings and tradespeople would change again, replaced by large office buildings, warehouses, and a new generation of workers.

Lower Hudson Street today is the apex of Tribeca, the Triangle Beneath Canal Street, a trendy neighborhood of nineteenth-century buildings converted to loft apartments. This building at Hudson and Reade streets is one of the few modern structures in the historic neighborhood. The area's cobblestone streets and large industrial spaces are home to many independent film studios. Actor Robert De Niro led the way downtown when he opened the Tribeca Film Center on Greenwich Street in 1988, soon followed by Miramax and a flood of smaller companies. The neighborhood now has a large cast of people in the film industry—actors, writers, directors, editors, sound technicians, and more—all living and working within walking distance of each other.

Once a residential area, Broadway south of Greenwich Village had become an active commercial district by the time of this 1860 view. The buildings reveal a type of architecture that became a major feature of commercial New York in the mid-nineteenth century—cast-iron construction. Developed in the 1840s, it soon transformed the facades of all kinds of buildings: department stores, offices, factories, and even warehouses. Not the boxy, utilitarian structures known today, these were built as well-proportioned buildings with large windows and the finely wrought details of Greek and Roman columns.

In the 1960s, as businesses moved out of the old buildings, the artists moved in, converting the large loft spaces to light-filled studios. The area was dubbed SoHo, South of Houston Street, a quirky neighborhood of businesses and residences. But it took some time before living in SoHo became legal. Today, decades after city inspectors evicted artists from industrial buildings, SoHo has become the city's trendiest neighborhood. Most of its remaining cast-iron buildings are protected by landmark laws, and the occasional vacant lot is snatched up quickly for luxurious new development. The building under construction, designed by French architect Jean Nouvel, will be one of the most expensive condo apartment buildings in New York. Residents will be able to enjoy the French Culinary Institute restaurant in the white cast-iron building across the street.

The scaffolding is still up in this 1889 picture of the wooden arch that was erected that same year to commemorate the centennial of George Washington's inauguration as the nation's first president. Paid for by the residents of the Washington Square neighborhood in Greenwich Village, it was painted white, ornamented with stucco wreaths, and topped by an eight-foot-high statue of Washington. The arch was so popular that a public subscription campaign was mounted to pay for a permanent marble version. The project presented a challenge, coming on the heels of the long campaign to fund the Statue of Liberty pedestal, but famed pianist Jan Paderewski gave it a boost by staging a benefit concert.

Both the wooden original and this marble version of the Washington Square Arch were designed by one of the best known and most prolific architects of the day, Stanford White, of the prominent firm McKim, Mead, and White. The permanent structure, built at the foot of Fifth Avenue, slightly south of the original location, was completed in 1895. Today, the arch is the quintessential landmark of Greenwich Village, so closely associated with the neighborhood that few people are aware of its connection to White or even George Washington. Although Washington's statue is no longer on top, two others appear on the reverse side of the arch, one sculpted by Alexander Calder.

Rising above the corner of Sixth Avenue and Tenth Street, the Jefferson Market Courthouse looks like a medieval castle out of place. A monument of American High Victorian Gothic design, it was created in 1877 on an old market site by Frederick Clarke Withers and Calvert Vaux, one of the designers of Central Park. The lower floors housed courts and a prison, and the bell tower served as a fire-watch station. Although municipal authorities were skeptical about its unusual design, a poll of architects in 1895 placed it fifth on the list of America's ten best buildings. In this 1960 view, the building was vacant and faced an uncertain future.

In 1959, a time when the historic preservation movement was still new, a group of New Yorkers organized a "Get the Clock Started on Jefferson Market Courthouse" committee to as a way to draw public attention to the building's precarious condition. They not only started the clock but also mounted a campaign to adapt the building as a public library. In a pivotal victory for preservationists, the building was converted to that use in 1967—one of the earliest adaptive reuse projects in America. With its clock still keeping time today, the Jefferson Market Branch of the New York Public Library is a prominent landmark in Greenwich Village.

Peter Cooper was an eclectic inventor, involved in everything from laying the Atlantic telegraph cable to producing edible gelatin, later known as Jell-O. Highly successful, but with little formal education, he established this building on Astor Place and East Eighth Street in 1859 as the Cooper Union for the Advancement of Science and Art, seen here in 1889. It was a novel undertaking, offering the first free, nonsectarian education to working-class men and women. The building was a unique engineering achievement that used a framework of steel railroad beams from Cooper's foundry. Its Great Hall hosted leading speakers of the day, notably Abraham Lincoln in 1860. Campaigning in the presidential election, Lincoln delivered a memorable speech here, establishing his antislavery platform.

True to its founder's wishes, Cooper Union still offers gifted students a free education in architecture, engineering, and fine arts. It is one of the most highly rated colleges in the country, and its Greenwich Village location, just east of Washington Square, has become one of the most desirable neighborhoods in the city. The elevated tracks in the earlier photo came down in 1959, opening the building to more light and air. It is the nation's oldest standing building that is framed with steel beams. The glass apartment tower built across the street from the school in 2005 has some of the highest-priced luxury condos in New York. The architect, Charles Gwathmey, taught at Cooper Union.

Located on a bend in Broadway, Grace Church stands out in this 1897 photo. It owes its prominent position to the stubbornness of a farmer who held onto his land when the city was laying out the street grid in 1811. Built in 1846, the graceful Gothic Revival church was designed by James Renwick years before he created the better known St. Patrick's Cathedral uptown. Partially visible on the right is a department store erected by A. T. Stewart in 1862. A cast-iron palace, it took up an entire block on Broadway between Ninth and Tenth streets. After Stewart died in 1876, the store lost business, but by the time of this photo, it was under new management. John Wanamaker bought it in 1896, built a magnificent addition on Eighth Street, and for the next fifty years made Wanamaker's the ultimate name in merchandising.

Recently restored, Grace Church is widely recognized as an architectural treasure. But the department store was destroyed in a spectacular fire that burned for two days in 1956. The apartment building that replaced it, behind the trees to the right, is appropriately named Stewart House. Wanamaker's addition, not visible in this photo, is still across the street on Wanamaker Place. It is now home to Kmart, the only New York City branch of this chain of discount stores. The tower to the right of the church steeple was built on top of the Con Ed Building on Fourteenth Street in 1926 to commemorate the lives lost in World War I.

Known for its workers' rallies and mass political protests, Union Square's history is closely tied to the rise of the Labor movement. But its name actually derives from its location at the union of two major roads, Broadway and Fourth Avenue. In this circa-1870 photo, the equestrian statue of George Washington, erected in 1856, is in the middle of Fourth Avenue at Fourteenth Street on the east side of the square. While this side was still residential, the west side was a bustling commercial and entertainment center. Macy's original department store and Tiffany's jewelry store were doing business there before they both moved to larger quarters uptown. The theater district also raised its curtain there before establishing its permanent home on Broadway and Forty-second Street.

Opened in 1839, Union Square Park has undergone several transformations. It was completely demolished in 1928 to make way for a large subway concourse. It emerged in 1930 with a new landscape and the statue of George Washington (inset) relocated within the park. Shabby and overrun by drug dealers in the 1970s, the park was completely refurbished in the 1980s and became a lively attraction as the home of New York's first—and now largest—farmers' market. The popular market has led to a boom in gourmet restaurants on the surrounding blocks. The statue of Washington still presides over the southern end of the park.

A close look at the writing on the large corner building in this 1892 photo reveals two popular aspects of late nineteenth-century entertainment. Over the ground-floor entrance is the name Fischer Pianos, a producer of high-quality pianos much in demand by America's rising middle class. Above the central arched window is the name of the publisher of the country's most widely read weekly magazine,

Frank Leslie's Illustrated Newspaper. Launched in 1855 as the first of its kind in the country, the publication was an enormous success until the depression of the 1870s. After Leslie's death in 1880, his wife, Miriam, brought the business back to profitability—hence the name Mrs. Frank Leslie on the building. She commissioned the architectural firm McKim, Mead, and White to build it in 1890.

Although hundreds of American piano companies flourished in the nineteenth century, few survive today. Fischer Pianos was one of the longest-running companies in operation, surviving from 1840 to 1982. Frank Leslie's publications no longer exist, but if Miriam Leslie, a lively and captivating woman, were alive today, she might buy some of the fashionable clothing now sold in the ground-floor space of her building.

She died in 1914 and left an estate valued at two million dollars to the women's suffrage movement. The arched facade of her building, destroyed in the 1970s, has been beautifully restored. Every other building in the older photo has been replaced, and the Empire State Building now rises in the background.

Rising like the prow of a great ship, the Flatiron Building was the first tall structure to soar north of City Hall. Built in 1903 on a triangular plot of land on Twenty-third Street between Fifth Avenue and Broadway, it replaced a group of much smaller, separate structures. As the only building on the site, it appears much taller than its twenty-three stories. It was officially called the Fuller Building, but soon became identified by its flatiron shape. On the right, the shorter building with a flat roof and awnings is the Fifth Avenue Hotel, the first one in the United States with elevators, then called "vertical railway cars." Opened in 1858, the hotel had an elegant dining salon where powerful politicians held court, and where Theodore Roosevelt advanced his career in the 1880s.

Surrounded today by taller buildings, the Flatiron's solitary stance on a triangular island still sets it apart and makes it one of New York City's most recognized landmarks. It also has newfound appeal as part of a trendy neighborhood, recently dubbed the Flatiron District. Located between Madison Square Park and Chelsea, the district is filled with restaurants, galleries, and condo apartments converted from old office buildings. The building's ornate terra-cotta facade, recently cleaned, can be appreciated once again. The Fifth Avenue Hotel is gone, demolished in 1908 and replaced by an office building.

Although this view focuses on an ornate streetlight at Madison Square, the object of greater interest is to the right. At the edge of Madison Square Park is the Statue of Liberty's hand and torch. Her dislocated limb was first displayed here in 1876 to raise funds needed to build her pedestal. The park, located across the street from the first Madison Square Garden (not visible in this photo), was an excellent place to attract public attention. Nevertheless, fundraising moved at a snail's pace, largely because it was seen as a project of wealthy New Yorkers. It succeeded only after *New York World* publisher Joseph Pulitzer made it an everyman's crusade, eliciting an outpouring of contributions from the newspaper's readers. The hand and torch rested for a decade in the park before being reunited with the statue in New York Harbor in 1886.

The ornate streetlight is gone and Madison Square Park bears no evidence of its historic connection either to the Statue of Liberty or Madison Square Garden, now a modern sports arena on West Thirty-fourth Street. Named for President James Madison in 1847, the park was spruced up in the 1870s with many different statues of famous Americans. It was refurbished again a few years ago through a fundraising campaign of its own, paid for largely by the insurance companies and other businesses surrounding the park. Reopened in 2001, it is a pleasant urban oasis and a popular lunchtime spot for local office workers. Ten blocks to the north, the Empire State Building has been part of the background since 1931.

Triumphal arches and pillars worthy of Roman generals were built on two separate occasions, twenty years apart, on the Fifth Avenue side of Madison Square. This one, called the Arch of Freedom, was built in 1919 to welcome soldiers home from World War I. A group of doughboys in uniform can be seen to the left. A similar monument, just as elaborate, had been built on the same site in 1899 to celebrate Admiral Dewey's victorious return from defeating the Spanish in the Battle of Manila. Both sets of monuments were only temporary structures, built quickly with plaster and lath.

The triumphal arches and all signs of their pomp and circumstance are long gone from Madison Square. The harsh reality of World War I overshadowed any desire to preserve the air of celebration that had marked the Arch of Freedom. The only remaining monument is the obelisk on the left (not visible in the earlier photo). Erected in 1857, it is dedicated to General William J. Worth, who fought in the Seminole and Mexican wars in the 1840s. It is also Worth's actual burial site, the only one of a public figure under a Manhattan street. Although he is also memorialized by Worth Street in Lower Manhattan, he is better known in Texas, where the city of Fort Worth honors his memory.

Brand-new in this 1905 photo, Macy's had just opened its doors here on Herald Square at Thirty-fourth Street and Sixth Avenue. Rowland Hussey Macy had opened the store in 1858 on Union Square, but he did not live to see it rise to its full glory. The men behind the move uptown were the new owners and innovative entrepreneurs, Isidor and Nathan Straus. They built this huge emporium on the site of Oscar Hammerstein's Manhattan Opera House, which moved farther uptown to establish a new theater district on Forty-second Street and Broadway. The Herald Square Theatre sign to the right of Macy's is evidence of the old theater district still in operation at this time. The Strauses failed to gain control of the entire site, as seen by the smaller corner building nestled within Macy's embrace.

Today, Macy's famous sign covers the corner building that the Straus brothers had failed to acquire. The company's red star logo harks back to the founder, Rowland Hussey Macy, a onetime whaler who had a red star tattooed on his hand. The first big department store to move north of Union Square, Macy's made Herald Square the city's busiest shopping district until the 1960s. Its former neighbor and biggest competitor, Gimbels, closed years ago, and the rise of Bloomingdale's on the Upper East Side attracted the city's wealthier clientele. But Macy's, still the best-known name in New York department stores, continues to draw crowds to Herald Square.

The luxurious Waldorf-Astoria was originally two side-by-side hotels built by feuding cousins of the Astor family. William Waldorf Astor built this one, the Hotel Waldorf, in 1893, overshadowing the next-door mansion of his despised aunt Caroline. Her son, John Jacob Astor, at first planned to demolish his mother's house and build stables to stink up his cousin's opulent hotel. But since their fortunes were tied together, John Jacob reconsidered and instead built the Astoria—an even larger, more splendid building—in 1897. The two buildings functioned as one hotel, but the cousins agreed that if their alliance fell apart, they could seal off the ground-floor connection.

The original Waldorf-Astoria Hotel died of thirst during Prohibition and was demolished in 1928 to make way for the Empire State Building. Both the Empire State and the new streamlined Waldorf-Astoria Hotel on Park Avenue and Fiftieth Street were completed in 1931. The Empire State Building broke all construction records, reaching 102 stories in fifteen months. Opened at the start of the Depression, it had no rivals for height but plenty of competition for office space. For years it was called "the Empty State" and survived on entrance fees to its lofty observation deck. Since the fall of the Twin Towers, it is once again the city's tallest building.

© 1923 By W.J. ROEGE N.Y.

This monumental, two-block-long classical temple was built from 1904 to 1910, a time when railroad stations became as expansive as their operations throughout the nation. To build its first station in New York City, the Pennsylvania Railroad cut a tunnel under the Hudson River in 1904, connecting the island of Manhattan to the rest of the country. Like Grand Central, the city's other great train station in construction at this time, Penn Station was an engineering and architectural marvel.

Designed by McKim, Mead, and White, it not only moved a complex transportation network through the city, it also celebrated it with a sense of civic grandeur. The grand waiting room with its great, arched windows rises above the huge building. Construction of the station cleared blocks of tenements in Hell's Kitchen and was heralded as the dawn of a new era for West Midtown.

Like the tenements it replaced, Penn Station fell victim to changing times and new property values. As automobiles outpaced train service in the 1960s, the railroad sacrificed its grand station to higher real-estate revenues. The station was demolished in 1963, replaced by this office tower and the new Madison Square Garden, a giant doughnut of a building built on the site of the grand waiting room. To sports and rock-concert fans, the Garden is the ultimate venue. To those who remember the original Penn Station, the modern building is a sorry reminder of the loss of a magnificent space. Although the station still operates beneath the Garden, the monumental building and its vast waiting room are only a memory. Their loss led to a public outcry and the creation of the city's first landmark protection law in 1965.

Like most of the large corporations of the day, the Pennsylvania Railroad looked to the architecture of classical Rome to express the scale of its vast empire. Charles McKim chose a perfect model for the station's interior in the ancient Baths of Caracalla. His design took the traveler through a long, carefully modulated system of magnificent arcades and corridors to the grand waiting room. Seen here in 1911, just a year after the station was completed, it was an awe-inspiring space of vaulted ceilings, towering columns, and arched windows that flooded the space with daylight.

The low-ceilinged space of the new station is more like a subway concourse than a train station. Although it is still the busiest train station in North America, Penn Station's cramped basement quarters, built in 1968, are a sad reflection of the decline of federal support for passenger rail service. Plans were announced in the 1990s to recapture some of the station's original elegance by moving it to the post office building across the street. Also designed by McKim, Mead, and White, the monumental building is no longer needed for postal services and has the same classical facade as the old station. The project still awaits financing and final approvals.

When the first Grand Central Depot was built at Forty-second Street in 1871, the area was at the northern outskirts of the city. Although critics complained that it was "neither grand nor central," the railroad had little choice in locating the terminal, since steam-powered locomotives and open tracks were banned south of Forty-second Street. This sprawling Second Empire building, enlarged in 1899, covered an enormous ground-level train shed with open tracks extending for blocks. Although a few pedestrian bridges were built over the tracks, the area to the north of the terminal remained noisy, dirty, and dangerous for many years.

The new Grand Central Terminal on Forty-second Street and Park Avenue was completed in 1913 as the crowning glory of Cornelius Vanderbilt's New York Central Railroad. Elevated on a platform above Park Avenue with a triumphal triple-arched facade, it became a grand gateway to New York City. Over the years, it was surrounded by much taller buildings and a constant flow of traffic. The glass building erected behind the terminal in the 1960s is the south face of the Met Life Building. Critics called it "a monstrous bland blanket" draped over the terminal. Nevertheless, Grand Central's historic facade, still crowned by the sculpture of Mercury and recently cleaned of soot, rises above the fray.

This classic photo is a stunning view of daylight streaming through the seventy-five-foot-high windows of Grand Central Station's main concourse. The splendid interior, designed as a superb embodiment of the station's monumental character, became the nation's premier public space. Towering columns rose to a vaulted ceiling painted with a mural of the constellations. Spotlights behind the ceiling illuminated the stars. Two teams of architects worked on the project: Reed & Stem and Warren & Wetmore. Whitney Warren, who got the job through the influence of his cousin, the railroad's chairman, William Vanderbilt, is nonetheless credited with much of the terminal's artistic achievement.

The main concourse is a glorious space today, thanks to a decades-long preservation battle that saved the terminal from destruction. With train service declining in the 1950s, the ceiling lights of the zodiac went out, grime stained the stone columns, and a giant screen advertising Kodak film covered one wall of the grand windows. The railroad at first tried to demolish the terminal, and when that failed they tried to build a skyscraper on top of it that would have pierced this room with steel columns. In 1978, after years of lawsuits, the U.S. Supreme Court upheld the terminal's landmark protection. Twenty years later, the Kodak screen finally came down, a marble staircase went up in its place, the cerulean blue ceiling was cleaned, and its stars were relit. Filled with bustling shops and restaurants, the concourse is again a vibrant place for tens of thousands of commuters.

The train yards pictured in this photo stretched many blocks to the north of the first Grand Central Depot at Forty-second Street. Ever since their creation in 1871, the open yards had been a death trap, killing and injuring people who lived along their borders. In 1902, after two trains collided in a steam-filled tunnel farther north, killing seventeen, the city required all railroads to switch from steam to electric-powered locomotives. By 1905, when this photo was taken, the new Grand Central Terminal was under construction, along with an ambitious project to place all of its new, electrified tracks underground.

The new Park Avenue, stretching for a dozen blocks north of the terminal, was built over the open train yards. Seventy new tracks were laid underground on two levels, supported by a submerged forest of columns. The project was the genius of New York Central engineer William Wilgus, who envisioned a new urban fabric—"a city within the city"—over the intricate track system. He also came up with a brilliant way to pay for it all, selling air rights above the tracks to developers.

They built Park Avenue's elegant office towers and hotels, many of them connected by underground passageways to the terminal. This is the Helmsley Building, built in 1929 as the opulent headquarters of the New York Central Railroad. Traffic passes through the arched portals at its base, circling the terminal on the other side before continuing south on Park Avenue.

Covering two blocks and holding twenty million gallons of water, this reservoir distributed New York City's first dependable supply of clean drinking water. A forty-mile-long aqueduct system built in 1842 brought fresh water here from the Croton Dam north of the city. By the time of this 1899 photo, a new, larger Croton aqueduct built in 1890 was carrying water to a bigger reservoir in northern Manhattan.

Plans to demolish the Forty-second Street reservoir and build a park in its place were made as early as the 1870s, when the new aqueduct was proposed. But neighboring property owners balked at paying taxes for the new park and defeated the city's plan in court. The old reservoir finally came down in 1899, soon after this photo was taken.

The New York Public Library, a classical temple of books, was built on the old reservoir site in 1911. The project was conceived in the late nineteenth century, at a time when municipal libraries were a civic luxury. It was realized in 1895 when three of the city's largest private libraries came together to contribute their collections and endowments. Andrew Carnegie provided most of the construction funds, and the architecture firm of Carrere & Hasings submitted the winning design. Private donors pooled their resources again in the 1980s and 1990s to restore the building's interior to its original splendor. A unique research facility today, its millions of books are housed outside of the building in multiple layers of stacks extending for miles under the adjacent Bryant Park.

The Art Deco spire of the Chrysler Building was a newcomer to the eastern end of Forty-second Street in 1930, the year the skyscraper won a frenzied race to become the world's tallest building. With the competing Bank of Manhattan tower growing higher each day at 40 Wall Street, Chrysler's architect, William Van Alen, hid the lancelike spire and raised it at the last minute, topping his rival by 121 feet. The victory was sweet but short-lived. The Empire State Building captured the title in 1931. This view shows Forty-second Street's older residents, the public library and Bryant Park, on the right, and across the street is the columned front of the Stern Brothers department store.

Glass-walled buildings, including the HBO headquarters in the foreground, now dominate the view. The swooping wall of the Grace Building replaced the Stern Brothers store in 1974. The unusual form was a unique and controversial response to the city's zoning requirement to set tall buildings back from the street. By the mid-1970s, the Chrysler Building, the gleaming embodiment of the jazz age, had fallen on hard times. With empty offices, cracked walls, and leaks in its dome, it was sold at a bank foreclosure. Fortunately, the new owner repaired the building, and a total restoration completed in 2002 brought it back to its shining, showy self. Sadly, the original architect's career was extinguished in the Great Depression of the 1930s. While his work has become one of the city's most beloved landmarks, Van Alen never designed another major building.

Once on the northern outskirts of the city, Forty-second Street was rivaling Wall Street as the skyscraper kingdom by the time of this view in 1930. The Chrysler Building, unmistakable with its long spire, had just been completed, joining a troop of towers marching up the street in the same period. To the right of the Chrysler is the Daily News Building, and to the left is the Chanin Building, both completed in 1929. Skyscrapers first appeared at Manhattan's southern tip because its narrow borders made vertical buildings an efficient way to add office space. But as tower after tower rose in Midtown, Manhattan's widest point, it became increasingly clear that efficiency was not the only incentive. Nearly every big business wanted a skyscraper to crown its success.

Residential buildings now rival office towers in height. The one rising between the Empire State and Chrysler buildings is the Trump World Tower, the tallest residential building in the world when it was completed in 2001. Although it looks taller from this view, its seventy-two-story shaft does not beat the height of the seventy-seven-story Chrysler Building or the 110-story Empire State Building. Located on First Avenue and Forty-seventh Street, it soars over every other residential building seen here, including the United Nations Plaza buildings, the two glass towers to the left, and the new pyramid-topped tower on the right. Taken from the east, this view also shows the relatively low-rise buildings of Roosevelt Island in the foreground.

Seen under construction in this 1949 photo, the United Nations Building reflected New York City's emergence after World War II as the international capital of the world. Surprisingly, New York nearly lost that title to Philadelphia, which was offering the UN a prime location while New York officials were promoting the 1939 World's Fair site in Queens. Just as the UN committee was about to approve Philadelphia, real-estate mogul William Zeckendorf offered the city this prominent parcel of land on Manhattan's East River waterfront. John D. Rockefeller Jr. purchased it for eight and a half million dollars and donated it to the city. A week later, the UN approved the site as its future home. The view of the Secretariat Tower also shows East River Drive under construction.

The Secretariat Tower is still a striking landmark on its East River perch. Inspired by the French architect Le Corbusier, it was New York's first glass curtain wall building, a type of construction that changed the face of modern architecture. However, now more than half a century old, it needs a total facelift. The renovation will require the construction of another building to house UN staff while work on the Secretariat Tower proceeds over the next several years. The low building projecting over East River Drive is the Dag Hammarskjöld Library, built in 1961 in memory of the UN's late secretary-general.

Times Tower, the new home of the *New York Times*, is nearly complete in this 1904 photo. Construction of the city's first subway line is also evident in the broken pavement and debris in the center of the street. This was the year the newspaper ventured uptown, from its longtime home on Newspaper Row, to this intersection of Forty-second Street, Broadway, and Seventh Avenue. The old location, opposite City Hall, had been the nerve center of the city, but *Times* publisher Adolph Ochs knew that the subway would bring rapid expansion. Ochs convinced the subway company to name the Forty-second Street station after his paper, and the area soon became known as Times Square. The horse-drawn carriage in the photo is one of many serving theaters that had moved into the area in the 1890s, but the new subway, which was operating by 1908, eventually cut into their business.

A century after the *New York Times*'s daring move to a remote location, Times Square is one of the busiest and most vibrant areas of the city. Like the Times Tower itself, the square is plastered with billboards. Filled with cars, taxis, and people at all hours, it has been the crossroads of the world for most of the twentieth century. But Times Square will no longer be the home of the *New York Times*. The paper had outgrown the tower by 1913 and moved to a nearby building just off the square on West Forty-third Street. It will move again in 2007 to a new building farther west on Forty-second Street.

Dressed in pink granite and crowned by a searchlight, the Italian Renaissance–style Times Tower was clearly the belle of Times Square in the first years of the twentieth century. The paper moved into its elegant new quarters on New Year's Eve of 1904 and celebrated the event with a fireworks display in the square. On New Year's Eve of 1908, the year of this photo, it launched New York's most famous tradition by lowering an illuminated ball from the tower at midnight. Every New Year's Eve since then, throngs of revelers have gathered in front of the tower to await the ball's descent.

Unrecognizable from its appearance in the early twentieth century, the Times Tower is now more of a billboard than a building. Although it sported neon signs in the 1920s, it was totally transformed in 1963 when the Allied Chemical Company reclad the building in a concrete and marble sheath. Like the older version, it was belted by a moving sign of flashing headlines, expanded in later years to giant video screens that now cover the entire building. Once the star of the show, the tower itself vies for attention with huge screens on every corner of Times Square.

As seen on New Year's Day 1930, Times Square was still in its heyday, bustling as much during the day as at night. More than seventy-five theater marquees flashed with the names of Broadway shows. The Howard Hughes production of *Hell's Angels* was playing in the theater on the right. The new film industry had added sparkling movie palaces in the late 1920s. Hollywood's first talking picture, *The Jazz Singer* with Al Jolson, had made its debut on Broadway in 1927. Songwriters in Tin Pan Alley, the concentration of music publishers in the area, were turning out tunes about New York that made the city into a national melody. However, this peak period would end with the beginning of the Great Depression.

In the 1930s and 1940s, burlesque and peep shows, penny arcades, and dime-a-dance halls transformed Times Square from the Great White Way to the capital of honky-tonk. By the late 1960s, prostitutes, drug trafficking, and adult movies had spread throughout the area, swallowing up or shutting down dozens of legitimate theaters. The survivors retreated to the side streets, but the sleaze followed—even

to the theater district's most famous address, West Forty-second Street. The neighborhood finally cast off its squalid past in the 1990s by means of a major investment of public and private funds. Restored theaters, new office towers, megastores, and family attractions have turned on the bright lights once again.

Seen from the seventieth floor of the RCA Building in Rockefeller Center in 1948, this view to the south is dominated by the city's tallest structure, the Empire State Building. The tower in the left foreground at Fifth Avenue and Forty-second Street was a precursor to the Empire State. Both were built by the architectural firm of Shreve, Lamb, and Harmon, a year apart in 1930 and 1931. The Empire State's original design called for a flat top, but the owners insisted on a distinctive spire as a mooring mast for dirigibles. Used only twice for that purpose, the spire became much better known when a giant gorilla climbed it in the original *King Kong* movie of 1933. The open space in the foreground is Bryant Park on Forty-second Street.

Without the World Trade Center towers (inset), the Empire State once again reigns over the sky. After the Twin Towers fell, the Empire State's lights were a patriotic red, white, and blue for nearly a year. Now back to their regular pattern of changing colors, they are a signal that even after a great tragedy, life in the city goes on. The Empire State's crown is New York City's beacon, a constant presence in the skyline, as familiar and comforting as an old friend. The smaller illuminated buildings are older landmarks—the New York Life Building (1928), left, and the Metropolitan Life Tower (1909), center left, both of which are visible in the earlier photo. Today, the Grace Building on Forty-second Street dominates the center foreground, blocking the view of Bryant Park.

The size of this vast undertaking in the heart of Midtown was mind-boggling, covering as much ground as thirteen Chrysler Building sites and providing as much office space as two Empire State Buildings. It was advanced by two of the most powerful businessmen in the country in the 1920s, John D. Rockefeller Jr., who had inherited his father's Standard Oil fortune, and Owen Young, the chairman of General Electric. The project was conceived as a grand home for a new metropolitan opera house, but its immense commercial nature overwhelmed the opera's backers and they pulled out, giving GE and its radio networks, RCA and NBC, the starring roles. Rising in construction on Sixth Avenue and Fifty-first Street in this 1932 view is the RKO Building, headquarters of one of the largest movie chains in the country.

Now Midtown's showcase, Rockefeller Center includes nineteen buildings between Fifth and Sixth avenues and Forty-eighth and Fifty-first streets—office towers, theaters, television studios, and restaurants, all connected to an underground shopping concourse and famous plaza. A team of architects designed the complex, but the central tower, originally the RCA Building, was principally the work of Raymond Hood. Its lobby walls were originally covered with murals by Diego Rivera, but were soon painted over because the Rockefellers objected to the artist's Marxist imagery. The fabled Rainbow Room restaurant is on the sixty-fifth floor. An observation deck offering spectacular views from the seventieth floor was closed for many years, but was reopened and renamed the Top of the Rock in 2005. Although the Rockefellers have sold a substantial part of the complex, it still bears the family name.

Radio City, the original name of the Rockefeller Center, also included this grand music hall on Sixth Avenue and Fiftieth Street. With 6,200 seats, Radio City Music Hall was the largest theater in the world when it opened in 1932. It began exclusively as a vaudeville stage but lost tens of thousands of dollars in its first two weeks of operation. It soon switched to movies, premiering *King Kong* in 1933. The combination of popular movies with live musical productions by the dancing Rockettes—originally called the Roxyettes after their first manager, Samuel "Roxy" Rothafel—kept the theater going for decades. Seen here in the 1950s, it was the city's premier showplace for movies and family entertainment.

By the 1970s, as the audiences for family movies and stage shows declined, Radio City Music Hall was losing business again. In 1978, the city was shocked by an announcement that the theater, with its striking Art Deco interior and famous rising sun stage, would shut its doors forever and be torn down. Saved at the last moment by state support, it has been beautifully restored. Now managed by the operators of Madison Square Garden, it has switched from movies to live concerts. At Easter and Christmas, the Rockettes return for their traditional holiday performances.

New York's Irish Catholic community was the city's largest immigrant group when construction of this grand cathedral on Fifth Avenue and Fiftieth Street began in 1858. Thousands contributed their nickels and dimes to make it possible, but a generation would pass before it was completed. Just two years after the foundation was laid, the work was interrupted by the Civil War and did not resume until 1869. Although the cathedral opened to visitors in 1877, the twin spires required additional funds and were not finished until 1888. During this thirty-year construction period, the neighborhood surrounding the cathedral changed from a raw outpost to a wealthy enclave. This photo was taken in 1894.

New Yorkers and tourists of all faiths flock to St. Patrick's today. Recognized as one of the city's great buildings, it stands out as a grand architectural achievement among more modern buildings. Rockefeller Center rose across Fifth Avenue in the 1930s, along with its statue of Atlas, which serves as a unique frame for the cathedral. St. Patrick's glass-walled neighbor on the left is the Olympic Tower, built in 1976 as one of the city's first luxury condominium buildings, combining expensive apartments with offices and shops below. St. Patrick's has hosted many of the city's most solemn and festive occasions, from the funeral of the slain Robert F. Kennedy in 1968 to the annual St. Patrick's Day Parade on Fifth Avenue.

As Central Park was nearing completion in the 1870s, Fifth Avenue was extended northward in a Gold Coast of palatial mansions along the park. By the time of this 1931 photo, a wave of new apartment buildings on Fifth Avenue—more than forty in the 1920s alone—had replaced many of the mansions. Despite the onset of the Depression, the area remained one of the wealthiest in the city. On the right is the Plaza Hotel rising above the park. In the center is the Crown Building with its pointed top. In 1929, the Museum of Modern Art's first gallery opened on the twelfth floor of this building, at Fifth Avenue and Fifty-seventh Street, before moving to its current home on West Fifty-third Street. In the far background is the newly completed Empire State Building.

Today, the view down Fifth Avenue takes in even larger office towers, many built in the real-estate boom of the 1980s. The glass slab behind the Plaza Hotel is the 9 West Fifty-seventh Street Building, wearing giant wind braces at its end. The low, white building in the center is home to the elegant Bergdorf Goodman store, built in 1928. The view of the Empire State Building in the earlier photo is now blocked by an office tower built behind the Crown Building in 1989. To the left, across Fifth Avenue, is the Trump Tower, built in 1983 and still home to Donald Trump and his popular TV show, *The Apprentice*. Next door, but out of sight, are the more sedate premises of Tiffany's, doing business here since 1940.

As the tower of this new hotel was under construction in 1927, a fire broke out in the wooden scaffolding and enveloped the upper part of the building. Fire department pumps could not reach the top of the thirty-eight-story structure and the water pipes in the building were not yet working. Crowds gathered in front of the building on Fifth Avenue and Fifty-ninth Street. Those who could afford it took rooms in the Plaza Hotel across the street to watch the spectacle. Fortunately, the fire burned itself out before causing any serious damage and the Sherry-Netherland opened later that year.

One of several skyscraper hotels built in New York in the 1920s, the Sherry-Netherland captured the title of the world's tallest apartment hotel. Today it is dwarfed by the taller and much bulkier General Motors Building, the white-and-black giant that replaced another elegant hotel, the Savoy, in 1968. But the Sherry-Netherland's distinctive tower still sets it apart. The crown and pinnacle give it the appearance of a French castle—a very tall one. Located across the street from Central Park, it offers stunning views and elegant accommodations. It was designed by Schulze and Weaver, the firm that created the new Waldorf-Astoria Hotel in 1931.

When the Plaza Hotel opened in 1907, it became New York's leading hotel. It captured that title from the grande dame of the 1890s, the first Waldorf-Astoria, by hiring its architect, Henry Hardenbergh, who made the Plaza his masterpiece. An older version of the Plaza had occupied this site since 1888, but the distinctive new building took full advantage of its premier location on Fifth Avenue and Fifty-ninth Street, across the street from Central Park. The expanse of open space sets it off like a giant château in the country. Its marbled lobby, the airy Palm Court restaurant, and the wood-paneled Oak Bar attracted the rich and famous. F. Scott Fitzgerald, a regular in the Oak Bar, immortalized the hotel in his novel *The Great Gatsby*.

Modern buildings now rise above the Plaza, yet the hotel still enjoys a special place in people's hearts. In the past, even those with quite different architectural preferences found it to their taste. In the 1950s, when Frank Lloyd Wright was designing the spiral-shaped Guggenheim Museum farther up Fifth Avenue, he always stayed at the Plaza. Another famous guest was the fictional Eloise, the children's book character created by Kay Thompson, who lived in a Plaza suite. But any future stories about Eloise may have to place her in a condo. Closed for renovation in 2005, the hotel is being transformed for the most part into luxury apartments. About a third of the building will remain as hotel rooms.

The largest public works project of the nineteenth century, Central Park was both an immense undertaking and a powerful demonstration of civic idealism. Its enormous size—843 acres—was an amazing commitment of undeveloped land to public use during a time of city expansion. Building the park took over twenty years, from 1856 to 1878. Directed by landscape visionary Frederick Law Olmsted and architect Calvert Vaux, over 20,000 workers blasted out rock, reshaped nearly three million cubic yards of soil, planted more than 270,000 trees, and built extraordinary park buildings. New Yorkers loved it, as revealed in this idyllic scene from 1894.

Today, Central Park is Manhattan's green heart, pumping renewed vitality into the nation's most densely built environment. It also is the city's lungs, filtering the air through an urban forest of trees. Twenty-five million people come to the park each year to enjoy its zoos, lakes, playgrounds, skating rinks, restaurants, and fifty-eight miles of pathways—or just to relax, as this sunbather is doing in the Sheep Meadow, a grassy respite from the concrete of the city. Designed as a romantic escape, the park has also become the world's largest natural garden, home to thousands of species of plants and animals.

Park designers Olmsted and Vaux were reluctant to insert hard surfaces into the park. But by setting this expansive, split-level terrace opposite the lake, they created one of the most scenic views to be found in the middle of a great American city. Its centerpiece is the Bethesda Fountain, topped by the winged *Angel of the Waters*, which celebrates the clean water supply first brought to the city by the opening of the Croton Aqueduct in 1842. The sculptor, Emma Stebbins, was inspired by a Biblical passage describing an angel who bestowed healing powers on the pool of Bethesda in Jerusalem. The terrace and fountain, completed by 1873, were a park showpiece in this 1893 view.

In the 1960s, the fountain became a hippie hangout, at times called "Freak Fountain." Physical abuse, made worse by continued neglect during the city's fiscal crisis of the 1970s, left the terrace scarred with graffiti, gouged carvings, and broken stairs. In the 1980s, the newly formed Central Park Conservancy raised funds to conduct a four-year restoration program, the beginning of a highly successful campaign to repair the entire park. Today, Bethesda Fountain, like the rest of Central Park, has been returned to its pristine glory. This is a "mirror image" of the archival photo, showing the other side of the double staircase. The statue of the angel, the most photographed monument in the park, was the inspiration for Tony Kushner's award-winning play, *Angels in America*.

The New York craze for ice-skating began during the hard winter of 1858, when Central Park's frozen lake was first opened to the public. Created out of a swamp, the twenty-acre lake opened long before the park was finished so that New Yorkers could have a place to enjoy boating and ice-skating—still a popular activity in this 1913 scene. In the right background is the Dakota apartment building on Central Park West and Seventy-second Street. Designed by Henry Hardenbergh, the same architect who later created the Plaza Hotel, it was built in 1884 as the city's first luxury apartment house.

Ice-skating has not been allowed on the lake since 1950, the year a safer artificial rink opened at the Fifty-ninth Street end of the park. Still a popular place for boating, the lake is a scenic setting framed by distinctive buildings. The Dakota, partially visible on the left, was once considered as remote from the city's fashionable districts as the Dakota Territory. Now joined by a phalanx of luxury apartment houses on Central Park West, it has been an elite address for years, particularly for entertainers and artists, including Leonard Bernstein, Boris Karloff, and Judy Garland. The former resident best known today is John Lennon, who was fatally shot in front of the building in 1980. The building with the twin towers is the San Remo, built in 1930 as the first of several prominent apartment houses designed for Central Park West by Emery Roth.

The woman sitting on this wharf, near a tenement neighborhood in the East Fifties, is looking north toward the towers on Sutton Place, a wealthy enclave perched on a bluff. The waterfront shown in this 1938 photo would soon be radically changed by the construction of East River Drive, a highway running the length of Manhattan's East Side.

Much of it was built during World War II with rubble from buildings bombed during the London blitz. Cargo ships returning to New York from England carried the broken masonry in their holds as ballast. It was later renamed FDR Drive in memory of President Franklin Delano Roosevelt, who died at the end of the war.

FDR Drive plowed through the old wharves and tenements near the river. Although the lower floors of one elegant apartment house lost their views and yacht landing, the highway was slipped under the riverfront gardens on Sutton Place. Today, the East Fifties section of the riverfront is all posh apartment houses, including many new ones that block the older towers. This photo was taken from a footbridge that crosses the drive at the end of East Fifty-first Street, leading to a riverfront esplanade. The Queensboro Bridge, opened in 1909 from East Fifty-ninth Street to Queens, appears in the background of both photos.

The intersection at the corner of Central Park and West Fifty-ninth Street became known as Columbus Circle on October 12, 1892. On that date, the 400th anniversary of Columbus landing in the New World, Italian Americans dedicated the marble column in the center of the circle. Two years later, they topped it off with the statue of Columbus. By the time of this 1921 view, the area was filled with buildings. Many of those pictured here—forty-four in all—would be leveled in 1956 for construction of the New York Coliseum, a convention center and twenty-five-story office tower housed in a bland, boxy structure.

The Coliseum became obsolete in 1986 with construction of the new Jacob Javits Convention Center on West Thirty-fourth Street. But plans to tear it down were delayed by years of controversy over the size and shape of its replacement. In a dramatic display of opposition to the first plan for a large tower, Jacqueline Kennedy Onassis led a line of protesters opening umbrellas in unison across the street in Central Park to demonstrate the long shadow the tower would cast. The city finally approved construction of the Time Warner Center shown here. It opened in 2003 with a luxury hotel, apartment and office towers, upscale shops, restaurants, and concert halls, all curving around the newly landscaped circle.

Tens of thousands of Americans lost their jobs in the panic of 1893, an economic depression that lasted for nearly a decade, sending many New York families to shacks like these along the northern fringes of the city. This is a view of Riverside Drive between West Eightieth and Eighty-first streets. Mansions like those in the far right background would later replace all the shanties. Frederick Law Olmsted's plan for Riverside Drive is apparent in this newly paved section planted with young trees along the Hudson River. But his 1880s design for Riverside Park, a rolling stretch of green on bluffs between the river and the drive, would not be fully realized until the 1930s.

Apartment buildings replaced most of the mansions on Riverside Drive in the early twentieth century. Despite a decline after World War II, the area has retained its cache and is particularly desirable because of its proximity to Riverside Park. In the 1930s, Robert Moses extended the park on a platform over the train yards bordering the river, doubling the size of Olmsted's plan. The trees on the left are part of this green ribbon of parkland that runs for more than sixty blocks along Riverside Drive. Its sloping lawns, terraces, woods, playgrounds, and sports facilities are heavily used and greatly valued by Upper West Siders.

CATHEDRAL & ST LUKES HOSPITAL B16922
MORNING SIDE PARK.
COPYRIGHT 1910 BY IRVING UNDERHILL NEW YORK.

After New York's Roman Catholic Irish community built St. Patrick's Cathedral, the socially prominent Episcopalians viewed it as a challenge, and made plans to build an even larger one—in fact, the largest in the world. The construction of the Cathedral of St. John the Divine on Amsterdam Avenue and 110th Street began in 1892 as a Romanesque design by Heins & LaFarge, as seen in its first stage on the left. By the time of this 1910 photo, Heins was dead, LaFarge had been fired, and a new architect, Ralph Adams Cram, was designing the rest of the building in the French Gothic style. To the right of the partially completed cathedral is St. Luke's Hospital, built in 1896 by architect Ernest Flagg at the start of his career, long before his signature work on the Singer Tower in Lower Manhattan.

More than a century after its ambitious beginning, St. John's is impressive but still incomplete. The ongoing work, visible in the scaffolding on the right tower, has outlived all of its major architects. Cram died in 1942 after completing the magnificent nave and west front with its great rose window and Gothic entrance. Work stopped when the United States entered World War II and did not resume until 1979. Although the cathedral will not be finished anytime soon, its architectural achievement so far is monumental. And despite its once imperious attitude toward immigrants, the congregation eventually opened its doors to people from all walks of life to become one of the most socially active groups in New York.

The avenue is named for James Lenox, a nineteenth-century philanthropist and book lover who established the Lenox Library, one of the great private collections that would later form the New York Public Library. His wealthy family had a farm on what is now the fashionable Upper East Side, far from this busy street in Harlem, shown here in 1930. Named by Dutch colonial settlers, Harlem began as a remote farming village and became an urban neighborhood in the late nineteenth century. African Americans began to live here in the early 1900s, seeking better housing and less racism than they encountered in other parts of the city.

Lenox Avenue is now Malcolm X Boulevard, renamed for the African American political and religious leader who was slain in Harlem in 1965. Harlem's population changed from predominantly white to black after the 1920s, and the neighborhood became the nation's center of African American economic, political, and cultural life. Modern buildings, including Harlem Hospital, seen on the left, have replaced those in the older photo. In recent years, Harlem's population has begun to shift once again. Driven by Manhattan's pricey real-estate market, white residents have been moving into the neighborhood, settling in the still-handsome brownstones on the side streets off this commercial intersection.

Many baseball fans from the 1950s remember the Polo Grounds, home of the New York Giants, as an ornate stadium on Eighth Avenue and 159th Street. But this site on Fifth Avenue and 110th Street is where the team first played and is where the more famous ballpark got its name. Actually built as a polo field, this site was first used for baseball in 1880. It contained two separate baseball fields divided only by a canvas fence and shared by two teams, the Giants and the New York Metropolitans. When both teams played home games, New York fans had to choose which one to watch. This photo was taken in 1886, three years before the Giants moved to another location. They eventually settled in the Polo Grounds on 159th Street in 1911.

Today, jazz, not baseball, is celebrated at 110th Street and Fifth Avenue. After the Giants left this spot in 1889, the field was reconfigured into city streets forming the northeastern edge of Central Park. It is now the site of the Duke Ellington Memorial, the first New York monument dedicated to an African American and the first Ellington memorial in the United States. The great jazz pianist once lived nearby. As for the famed Polo Grounds on 159th Street, the Giants left that stadium for San Francisco in 1957. The last team to play at the Polo Grounds was the New York Mets, the reincarnation of the New York Metropolitans, in 1963. The Mets moved to a new stadium in Queens in 1964 and the Polo Grounds were demolished to make way for apartment buildings.

A startling design in its day, this bridge over the Hudson River to New Jersey was the first one without any ornament. Opened in 1931, the 3,500-foot-long span—more than twice the length of the Brooklyn Bridge—was all bare steel, without any cladding or architectural flourishes. However, it was not planned this way. Its engineer, Othmar Ammann, and architect, Cass Gilbert, had intended to sheath the towers in granite. But as the Depression squeezed the project's budget, the steelwork was left exposed, to the delight of the modernist architect Le Corbusier, who called it the most beautiful bridge in the world. This view is a close look at the powerful steel cables strung through the top of the Manhattan tower and held in place by a huge anchorage.

The longest suspension bridge in the world when it was built, the George Washington lost that title to the Golden Gate Bridge in 1937. But as the only New York City bridge across the Hudson, rising more than 200 feet above the river, it has a commanding presence that can be seen for miles. Its graceful silhouette, rising here above the trees of Fort Washington Park at 178th Street, is an unmistakable sign to travelers arriving from the north that they have entered Manhattan. One of seventy-six bridges crossing the waters of New York City, it is one of the most recognizable.

INDEX